Mr. Plant Expert

by Sidney Allen
illustrated by Dominic Catalano

Core Decodable 108

Mc Graw Hill Education

Bothell, WA • Chicago, IL • Columbus, OH • New York, NY

MHEonline.com

Send all inquiries to:
McGraw-Hill Education
8787 Orion Place
Columbus, OH 43240

ISBN: 978-0-02-138072-5
MHID: 0-02-138072-4

Printed in Canada.

9 10 11 12 KOD 24

Kids and adults filled the hall. They came to see Mr. Plant Expert. They came to have fun.

"Hi! I am Mr. Plant Expert. Ask me about plants and gardens. Maybe you can stump me!"

"Mr. Expert," said a pupil. "I heard about a truck farm. Do huge trucks grow there? Are buses and cars grown there, too?"

"No," smiled Mr. Expert. "Veggies grow on truck farms. The veggies are cucumbers, beans, and so on."

"Farmers pack veggies in boxes. Trucks take the veggies to stores. That is why the farms are called truck farms."

"Is this true?" asked a boy. "Do plants get fuel from the sun? How can a hose reach that far?"

"Plants do get fuel from the sun," explained Mr. Expert. "But plants do not use hoses. Sunshine provides plants with fuel and energy."

"Bugs eat plants," said a man. "But do plants eat bugs?"

"A few do," said Mr. Expert. "They are good to take to picnics."

"My mom said you have a green thumb. Can I see it?" asked a cute kid.

Mr. Expert chuckled.

"I am a good gardener," explained Mr. Expert. "That is what a green thumb means. But my thumbs are not really green."

"There is a brick plant in town," said a boy. "Can bricks grow on plants?"

"No," said Mr. Expert.

"Plant can mean factory," said Mr. Expert. "A factory makes things. A brick plant makes bricks."

"Do plants like music? What tunes do they like?" asked a girl.

"Plant experts like music," said Mr. Expert. "I like rock tunes."

Mr. Plant Expert looked at the clock.

"Thanks, kids! Thanks, adults! I must run to pluck some weeds. See you next time!"